MW01157037

The Sea Glass Sisterhood

There is a secret sisterhood

of those who love the shore

and stroll along its sandy trails,

eagerly searching for

the jewels that the tides create,

with their persistent waves

those treasures sparkling in the surf,

each of us dearly craves.

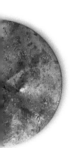

We share the understanding that

days at the seaside bring,

aware the bond between us all

is strong and shimmering.

At beaches found around the world,

we recognize our kin —

it's not our age, or looks, or size;

we may be plump or thin.

What matters is the way we move,

gaze fastened to the ground,

slowly becoming one with the

sensations that surround

this place of ever-changing charms,

which prompts us to feel whole

and, even in its wildest moods,

touches our very soul.

Our eyes glint like the glass we hunt,

algae and eelgrass green,

gray as the rocks, brown as the kelp,

blue as the noon-sky sheen.

An ancient impulse drives us on

to gather and collect

what others have regarded trash,

broken, discarded, wrecked.

We see the miracle in each

transformed, perfected shard,

perceive the message it contains

can lighten any heart.

The images stored in our minds

are of a certain kind,

the glorious, spectacular

once-in-a-lifetime find:

The vintage marble that did seal

a carbonated drink;

the chunk of well-cooked, frosted teal

without a single chink;

the plain-white bits the sun has kissed,

now lavender and pink;

the multies that seem painted with

brush strokes of brilliant ink —

small accidental works of art;

the bottle stopper stems,

relics of customs long bygone;

and many other gems;

smooth pieces of old pottery,

their porcelain as white

and delicate as the remains

(constructed from calcite)

of shells, and stars, and sanddollars,

the coastline puts on show,

those creatures born in salty streams,

sustained by ebb and flow,

which give us glimpses of the realm

that stretches out below

the smooth or roughish surface view,

where few of us may go.

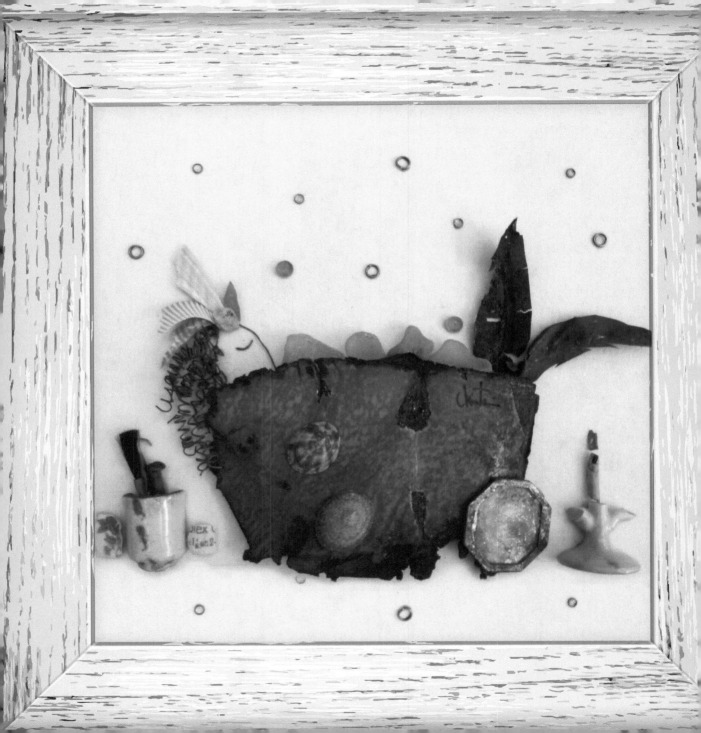

Yet, don't we all from time to time

indulge in daring dreams

of iridescent scales and fins

and underwater schemes,

in ocean depths, soothing and cool,

of which one seldom hears,

where fish-tailed women spend their lives

and cry their happy tears?

Admit it, you would want to be

a mermaid for a while,

explore the wonders of the blue

that does stun and beguile

us when we stand ashore and watch

the sun's light skip and whirl

in dots of brightness on the sea,

each like a shiny pearl.

Whether you walk the waterline

in regions of the north,

rugged, chillblained, and swept by gales,

where nightly skies bring forth

displays of dazzling color flares,

or visit southern coasts,

some tropical scenario

with frilly palms that boasts

turtles and dolphins floating through

clear turquoise lagoons,

and wooden chests in sunken ships

bursting with gold doubloons;

or if you merrily frequent

a somewhere in between

that is in many seasons quite

remarkably serene;

whether you are an islander,

or dwell at a large lake,

or comb the borders of a whole

big continent to take

away your own quota of joy

and splendid solitude,

and a well-tumbled, marvelous,

glossy and gleamy loot;

whether you have to brave the rain,

feet stuck in rubber boots,

or hail July in one of your

becoming bathing suits;

whether you greet me at the beach,

or quietly walk by,

if you love sea glass like I do,

we're sisters, you and I.

CHRISTINA GRAY

is an assemblage artist who finds beauty in the broken. She draws inspiration from her faith, transforming what was trashed, torn, and discarded into amazing works of art. Her materials are mermaids' tears, surf-tumbled pottery, scraps of metal, and other old sea debris, together with shells, driftwood, and pebbles, found on her frequent beachcombing and mudlarking trips; she loves to hunt for the next exciting treasure that will tickle her imagination. The collages she creates are playful, often whimsical, and always utterly charming.

Christina lives in a small town in rural Georgia with a spectacular natural vantage point, from which, as myth has it, you can see seven states. She loves to spend time with her children and grandchildren, is a passionate cook, and enjoys the company of her pet chicken, Sybil.

Find out more about Christina and her art at

instagram.com/bornagainbits

SILKE STEIN

is the author of the women's fiction novel *Foam on the Crest of Waves*, a captivating blend of mystery, romance, and mermaid yarn, set at one of the world's most famous glass beaches. She has also written two middle-grade books, and a volume of poetry titled *My Heart Sings to the Sea*, perfect for all who find joy, solace, and inspiration at the shore. Having been an avid reader since childhood, Silke took the detour of becoming a graphic designer before she discovered her passion for writing.

Silke lives at the south tip of beautiful Vancouver Island with her husband and her ever-growing sea glass collection. Long morning walks at the coast supply her with time for prayer, surf-tumbled gems and shells, photos of the pretty things she can't take home, and ideas for her next writing projects.

Find out more about Silke and her books at

silkestein.jimdo.com

Dear Reader,

or may I say Sister? As you have made it to this page, you are surely a member of the 'sisterhood'. I hope you have enjoyed Christina's artwork and my poem.

This book is very much a three-women show — the third being graphic designer Maria Ayala from California who assisted me (due to an eye problem my screen time is very limited) with skill, patience, and a lot of 'fancy footwork'. *¡Muchas gracias, hermana!*

The Sea Glass Sisterhood is the first of what we hope will develop into a small series of gift books for all who love sea glass, beachcombing, and having a good time at the shore.

Please support us by recommending *The Sea Glass Sisterhood* to others, giving it a rating or review, and stay in touch by subscribing to our newsletter and following us on Instagram and Facebook.

Check out our website for information and up-coming releases: *beachurchinbooks.ca*

Thank you very much,
and happy sea glass hunting!

Silke Stein